I Wish I Could be Peter Falk

UNIVERSITY OF CALGARY
Press

I Wish I Could be Peter Falk

Paul Zits

Brave & Brilliant Series
ISSN 2371-7238 (Print) ISSN 2371-7246 (Online)

© 2022 Paul Zits

University of Calgary Press
2500 University Drive NW
Calgary, Alberta
Canada T2N 1N4
press.ucalgary.ca

LIBRARY AND ARCHIVES CANADA CATALOGUING IN PUBLICATION

Title: I wish I could be Peter Falk / Paul Zits.
Names: Zits, Paul, 1978- author.
Series: Brave & brilliant series, ISSN (print) 2371-7238, ISSN (ebook) 2371-7246 ; no. 23.
Description: Series statement: Brave & brilliant series, ISSN (print) 2371-7238, ISSN
    (ebook) 2371-7246; no. 23 | Poems.
Identifiers: Canadiana (print) 20210306610 | Canadiana (ebook) 2021030667X | ISBN
    9781773852393 (softcover) | ISBN 9781773852409 (PDF) | ISBN 9781773852416 (EPUB)
Classification: LCC PS8649.I87 I2 2022 | DDC C811/.6—dc23

The University of Calgary Press acknowledges the support of the Government of Alberta
through the Alberta Media Fund for our publications. We acknowledge the financial
support of the Government of Canada. We acknowledge the financial support of the
Canada Council for the Arts for our publishing program.

Alberta
Government

Canada

Canada Council   Conseil des Arts
for the Arts   du Canada

Printed and bound in Canada by Marquis
♻ This book is printed on 70lb Opaque Cream paper

Editing by Helen Hajnoczky
Cover image: Colourbox 17389171
Cover design, page design, and typesetting by Melina Cusano

Contents

for Me (& Ryan Gosling)

In the end, I admire the great philosophers only as I admire the celebrities in my gossip magazines. Their brilliance is only the equivalent of a celebrity's beauty; their integrity only the fervour of an ingénue's rise to fame. My stupidity places them at an infinite and glamorous remove.

—LARS IYER, from *Exodus*

Sometimes when I'm sad I picture a sleepless Benedict Cumberbatch freeing a tiny sparrow.

—MICHAEL SCHULMAN

I'm not confident enough to just create work.

—GARETH WRIGHTON

Once You Push the Button

A lot of these things feel like quotes that you've said, but you haven't said them.

—RYAN GOSLING

The perfect Canadian pores

"You have the perfect

Canadian pores,

like the rain of joyful

tiny yellow hairs

on a bee's body,"

she says.

"It's like watching passengers

tumble down

slanted decks."

I look out

onto my dawn-simulating

nighttime blackout-shading system.

Muscular angels

unfold my brow.

I look up and out,

the world, this kind of

rising spectacle

like walking the edge

of a circus.

Once you push the button

I brush my teeth

basking in a blaze

of Spielbergian cinematography.

See! My features are nearly still

in the changing light.

See! See!

My corona turns out

the most sublime shadows.

I blot a drop from my nose.

Today I will author guidelines

on how to create mistrust

between friends, and

if there is time:

How to bring about systemic

professional and personal

social failure.

Like any religion,

once you push the button

the system must work forever.

She loves with a force

She loves with a force

that can shatter seashells,

aquarium glass.

Even the eel skinner

seems reborn.

"You are being taken back

by nature," she says

of my catlike whiskers

and glowering eyes.

Like petals,

they are precisely shaped

and rippled

to receive the light

from a star.

We stand in the blaze

of maple leaves veined

by a crooked lattice of trunks,

her hands

down my sinister-looking *V*

the glint off her teeth

like the twinkle

of glowing plankton

disturbed by charging sperm whales.

Terminal rustzone

The streets are yellow with a long,

long sunset.

Everything looks

like it was sand once.

Yellow lights cropped

at the ankle.

I am coughing

in the suburban sun,

coughing in this terminal

rustzone.

The cars

are pulling themselves

into small, tight curls.

"Let's go somewhere

with roller coasters,"

she says.

"Somewhere where people

are breaking into song

and dancing

and flying in the stars."

Her fingernails

are like florid Japanese gelatin.

And they are pushing my heart

into the cold inside

of its passenger door.

I sip my water

I sip my water.

It tastes utterly
ordinary.

She is practicing her playfaces,
backlit
by a milky blue sky.

Her cell phones rings
to music from *Grey's Anatomy.*
"I can't stand the scent
of my Motorola phone,"
she says.

Her evil eye

is like a girl's failing

artificial heart valve.

It is not quite noon

but I have nevertheless

nearly exceeded

my daily activity budget.

My little self repair

I make her bed

every morning,

which helps lower

our relationship stress.

I am making

peak performance

my goal.

She holds up the hand

she's just cut

opening a water bottle.

"When we start with a torture chamber

everything's uphill from there,"

she says.

Today has its thorns.

It is as if there are two middle-

aged Russian brothers

with the minds of infants

between us.

There is a scab on my shin

surrounded

by pink tissue.

My little self repair

is almost complete.

Where the f— are you?

She playfully texted me:
"where the f— are you?
I've been waiting out here
for seconds and seconds!"

I imagine her windowpane plaid
wave of giggling.
It feels like blood returning
to a limb
after it's fallen asleep.
It feels like walking out
of a dark theatre.

Looking in the mirror
is like seeing a porn film
come on by mistake.

Looking in the mirror

is like looking out a window

and seeing every treetop

bending

in the same direction,

the blue sky shining,

as if newly made.

Or, if it's nighttime,

like stars bleeding to life

in a sky suddenly

too small to hold them.

A fireball of charisma

I have a nervous system

made from Christmas lights

with the glow

of one hundred full moons.

I am a fireball of charisma.

Think of a giant flower

in space

unfurling itself.

My veins are tiled with lightbulbs

crushed like paper planes

in King Kong's paws,

and so on.

Right now I'm into colour.

Like this purple jacket

from Canada Goose.

I'm into statement socks,

and cargo pants

with pockets big enough

for a peacock to turn.

She reads Dan Brown

"How do you hard-boil an egg again?"

she asks.

She reads Dan Brown,

attends Pink concerts,

and orders Philadelphia rolls.

She favours

bejewelled skull patterns

and fabrics with a sheen.

She is fond of the word cuddle

"because it really is

what it sounds like."

Her bangs are tough

and sweet at the same time.

She believes that perfumes

have decades attached to them—

that with them

come the memory

of old family photos.

I am the perfect bonfire

for burning marshmallows.

But her brain runs on cylinders

mine doesn't even have.

If she were a millipede

She is trying to produce

the ultimate selfie.

But she looks vulnerable,

like a deer

framed in a hunting

riflescope.

If she were a moth

she'd be holding her abdomen

upright

and posing as a twig.

If she were a millipede

she would be ready

with a mouthful of cyanide.

She is in a state

of permanent visibility.

She is going for something

between a kitten

and a beheading.

Today I'd like to nudge her

with a glass stick.

She is as delicate

as a mad bomber,

and as graceful

as an act of God.

A billion Google images

My dreams forge ghostly cicadas

out of the sunlight

jacketed in steel.

I am a natural raconteur—

And I can also clean your clock.

I make tables from church doors.

I am a little sport, a little

street, with graphic knits

with the pixelated worlds

of the Mario Brothers.

I feel a need to search out

your weaknesses.

Today I avoid spreading my data

as much as possible. I carry

a billion Google images

in my head

at a time.

The answers

to a child's questions

matter to me,

but like a fingerprint

under Sherlock's gaze.

Let's Talk Sweatpants

But what if it had your brains and my looks?

—George Bernard Shaw

Let's talk sweatpants

Let's talk sweatpants.

My clothes are comfortable
but they make me aspire
to more.

"There's that great
Coco Chanel quote
about getting completely dressed
and taking one thing off,"
she says.
"You will be more comfortable
in a soft structure,"
she adds.

I am crouching,

execution-style,

and there is a kind of movement

interpreted in my fabric,

my endorsement-worthy

hair.

I quickly flag

a distracting crease

to remove later.

I am going to roll my sleeves up

and take care

of this situation.

Like a deep-sea vent

My face

is a curious business.

Like a deep-sea vent.

It's like reeling in

a barn door.

It's firing up

the whole imagination

of India!

I rehearse raising

my inner eyebrows.

One at a time.

I pull down my lip corners.

"What does

a positive emotion

look like?"

I ask her.

She looks over me

like a jeweller.

Like she's observing

the radio glow

of the milky way.

Searching my eyes

for flecks

from exploded stars.

I am becoming keenly aware

of the cyclops-like glares

of the lampposts.

The Smart-billboards

tailoring ads

to my appearance.

I hear camera clicks

coming from outer space—

I hear them through

the celestial dust.

Minutes later,

the moon blocks the sun.

My best friend

Two words, I say to my dog:

cashmere lining.

My bombproof tote

I finished watching *First Blood*

while you were falling asleep

on the couch.

I am not able to separate

those realities—

it will change the vibration

in the room.

My engines of sight

whirr to life.

"The snipers," I say,

"are in the bell tower,

waiting."

Outside,

a big black dog and its small master

run by the flame-blackened

vacant houses

across the street.

There is dark and strange stuff

sloshing inside of me,

and only an exit sign glows

in the distance.

The movie is finished

and if I had hats

I'd be throwing them in the air.

Glasses are an emotional thing

I want to drive off barefoot

in a Lincoln Sedan

with a booster seat

in the back,

wearing glasses that channel

Gregory Peck's specs.

I want to stomp

the fuckin' streets

and find chainlink fences

that are bent

from where the kids jump over.

I love my girls

in a Brontëan pallor

with Red Nail Extensions

in Jazzy Doll

Frog Prince Lip Gloss

and La Laque Couture

in Savage Pink.

The military trend is big.

I am indelicate,

as strong as you'd think

and quiet to a fault.

My fridge lets me know

if I need milk

while I'm at the grocery store:

"Ze-roooo," it says.

The *o* syllable has a long tail,

and a face like a sheep.

For Shia LaBeouf

My face.

There is no bad angle on it.

I stand out like a spaceship
among adobe huts.

My neckline has an
end-of-the-world vibe.

Today I am searching
for ancient light—
looking for a purpose-built backdrop
for Instagramming
a sun salutation.

I imagine that a few blocks away,

Shia LaBeouf

is on a sixth-floor patio

overlooking a historic landmark.

Make it better,

says the demonic little voice

inside his head.

He has a joy that I'd love to adopt.

It's all about exploring futuretopias

My face.

It has an
anthemic appeal.

It moves comfortably
and doesn't wrinkle.

It can break up
the silhouette of animals.

So I need a suit
with a reservoir of potential.

I need a suit that I can wear
to a marketing meeting
with a 23-year-old creative,

or a power-lunch

on a Wednesday.

I need a suit that I can wear

to a surreal,

Little Tokyo

mini-mall.

A popping-up-in-front-of-dark-

curtains-coloured suit

to go with a wedge

of canned smile.

I need something for the nonstop

surveillance cameras

scowling at me,

capturing the Zeitgeist.

Time to musk up

I am choosing between two

crewneck sweaters:

one with pictures of the

California wildfires,

the other with Chelsea Manning-leaked

images of US soldiers firing

at Iraqi civilians.

Even when it's make-believe

this land is dangerous.

"I like your citrus-forward

amber-driven fragrance,"

she says.

"But the heart-of-iris finish

feels reckless."

She makes a rough kind of sense.

Our conversation

is a Tetris game

come to life.

"If you're going to the ball

you might as well slay,"

she concludes,

the words GUCCI DOWN 2 THA

hand-painted on her tights.

It is a tremendous cognitive load

to consider.

For Neil Armstrong

for Kyle Flemmer

I hated being a kid.

I just didn't like
the way it felt.

"I have a limited amount of time,
and, you know,
I've got to get started,"
I told my teachers.

We are watching Neil Armstrong
kick up a little moondust.
I would like to see less

luxury mediocrity

with the spacesuit.

Turbulence makes her giggle,

she says.

But space also has a dark side.

Plans for asteroid mining

seem to have stalled a bit.

"If you can't look out the window

why go?"

she asks.

I need something to impress.

Like that satisfying puff

of space dust.

I hated being a kid.

I just wanted it

to be over.

And now,

I want to be thought of

whenever a Chinese rocket

re-renters the atmosphere.

For Nicholas Cage

I want to puncture

my own mythos,

so I am practicing my Sam Shepard-

like trances.

I have set out

to out-alpha them all,

like a tower

weaponized by the sunshine.

Even my hair is confident,

flicked

like a meringue peak.

It looks snapped on,

and welded into place.

It is the purest crystallization

of ego,

like those neat pyramids.

It has one of consumerism's

most irresistible cocktails:

real-world practicality, with

a shot of lifestyle fantasy.

I carry it

like it's the antidote

to the zombie apocalypse.

A clutter of memorabilia

"I like to read

when the winds are light,"

she says.

Her eyes have a lounge-like

spaciousness

and remind me

of my first experiences

of water.

"And I like vampires.

They're sophisticated,

and knowledgeable,

and mysterious,"

she continues.

I am doing breathy

morning squats

in tube socks and underwear.

She wonders which one-piece

will make a statement poolside,

and cheerily dives

into a jackfruit taco.

I have stepped into my

memory archive,

a clutter of memorabilia,

where I run around a forming cloud,

coaxing it into shape.

A Thinking-woman's Fetish Object

All it comes down to is: I feel like shit but look great.

—BRET EASTON ELLIS, from *American Psycho*

I am a thinking-woman's fetish object

She sits close,

a giant planet

crammed up against its star.

A leg peeks out

from beneath the folds

of her dress.

She tells me about a roach

that if stung in the brain

by a wasp,

will follow it into a hole

where the wasp lays its eggs.

The roach is sealed inside

and left to be food

for its larva.

"You don't say,"

I respond

with just the right amount

of frisson,

but with my eyes at half-mast.

I am manufacturing a ceaseless

ta-da.

The camera

has to remain reverent.

I am a thinking-woman's fetish object,

I think.

First I'll make her forget

the days of the week.

Next, she'll forget about life

on Earth.

Miserable while laughing

We had Christmas and wrapped presents.

We had birthdays and made cakes.

We would have whole days

just dedicated to fighting.

Today the leaves crunch underfoot

like we are stepping on old

sea lion bones.

We are on our way to a mall

where we think a lemon-tree orchard

should be,

for its Instagrammability.

She wants a restaurant

that doubles

as a marine research lab.

We had argued

earlier in the walk

to a pulse-pounding musical score:

"If you're wearing high-end sweats

the kicks should match,"

she had said.

Her words are like smudge marks

left by museumgoers

pressing their foreheads

against the glass.

Black-and-white psychodrama

You and me,

we share some architecture,

sure,

some hardware,

but we are dramatically

different beasts.

I am muscled

like a Viking wagyu steer.

My elderly neighbours like me

because my strong hands

can open jam jars.

I am the Idris Elba

of the boy-next-door.

But I am impatient

for bloodshed.

I smell of machine oil

and fibreglass resin.

I curse double-yellow

no-pass zones.

This naturally cool exterior

hides barely contained veins

of savagery.

A flash from a drone overhead

illuminates the sparse

black-and-white

psychodrama

growing from my yawning

smile lines.

Genteelly distressed

I tell her that Hans Zimmer

composed my electric engine noise.

"Who?" she asks.

Grooming keeps my stress levels low.

I memorize shapes more easily

because colour

doesn't distract me.

Mine was the most intelligent embryo.

Now I'm somewhere in the middle,

somewhere between Kong

and Iglesias.

With me comes an atmosphere,

my own weather:

buildings reduce

to cracker crumbs.

I'm trying to find a way

to express something

about loneliness

and make it feel sexy

and immortal:

drinking rainwater

squeezed from moss.

I am a crime story in search

of a moral center.

I gravely stand in the middle

of this old regime

with a bigger toy

than yours

and a line of edible figurines.

A very un-moonlike rain

When I was young

I would pass evenings

in vacant lots

looking up at the sky.

I just wanted to leave

a tiny something

on the lunar surface.

I get dressed while reading

and clicking

through emails.

Today it is raining.

A very un-moonlike rain,

crackling

like walkie-talkies.

Later tonight,

when I put my feet

over the seat in front of me

in the movie theatre,

my shoes

will be harmonious.

It is my birthday.

And before anything

even happens,

an unmistakable smell

hits me.

Slightly burned,

slightly metallic.

The smell of sparklers,

the smell of space.

For Albert Einstein

A stubbornly bright beam of light

shines in from the corner

of the glass door.

She eats ice cream out of her new

Star Wars ramekin.

"Lets go wipe some hummus,"

she says.

We choose a place with a lobby mural

by Lichtenstein,

and I feel the kind of sad you feel

looking at the microscope slides

displaying slices

of Albert Einstein's brain.

The waitstaff are dressed

in rabbit costumes.

This evening she will unspool

a paranoid worldview

on fluoridation.

I will order a glass of goat milk

containing spider-silk protein.

The morels on our pizza

will remind me of the microscope slides

displaying slices

of Albert Einstein's brain.

No wider than a pinstripe

The skyline muscles

into the sunset.

Sauntering up to a cheerleader

with an explosion of straw-

coloured curls,

my sentences form themselves

and break apart

before they are even spoken.

She likes my rugged stitching.

"Pleats are your friend,"

she says.

We quick-scroll down

her Instagram timeline,

the space between us

no wider than a pinstripe,

skinny, like a blink.

The radio music

of the cosmos

becomes veils of wingbeats

on our cheeks.

A telephone bidding war

She is like water

that takes the colour

of whatever riverbed

it flows over.

She asks to be wooed

with picnics and jokes.

Wants her Ethiopian flatbread

cooked with burning sheep dung.

She wears her jewelry tucked-in.

She gushes

with vigorous brushstrokes,

thick pigment,

rambunctious shapes.

She activates

my default mode network.

Golden light rings her body.

She is like something

that you would win

in a telephone bidding war.

Like something

that should be surrounded

by volcanic black rock

for miles around.

For Willem Dafoe

I am part Mr. Darcy,

part cyborg,

part Milwaukee factory worker.

And I eat my fritters shirtless.

It's just me and my nice jawline.

"I really need to start making changes

right now," I say,

in the manner of Pope Francis.

My gestures carry weight.

I am a sort of Superman:

I don't laugh

I don't cry

I don't sleep calmly.

I want my pecs to be

much-papped.

My malevolence

too slippery to catch.

There are no secrets in my work,

didn't you know?

This is like a diary.

There are only so many time machines left.

A burglary scene

Tonight

we are acting out a burglary scene

before engaging in intercourse.

She wants love-making

in the age of missions

to Mars.

"You should stick me in the Batsuit,"

I say.

She looks too pleased

with herself

when she smiles.

She screams

when she should be whispering,

explodes

when she should be sitting still.

She wants to be super-'right now,'

Princess Diana in an

American football letterman.

She wants my watch face

made out of meteorite.

My dog prefers me in my

green nylon bomber

from Prada.

The magic dust?

My expertly managed

surface language.

My jacket that compresses

into its own pocket.

I zip up

I zip up

and turn my back on the sea.

I'm going Uncle Buck tonight,

with an oversized coat

and cigar.

Today

she was measuring her childhood

through the deaths

of different forms

of social media.

She wants to start micro-dosing

ayahuasca,

for the "ego death,"

she says.

I'm practicing looking

at a distant point.

There is a net of darkness

hanging

at the end of the block.

I will repeat the words over

and over again, until

my own name

sounds like

just someone I know.

Sources

Book Title

The title *I Wish I Could be Peter Falk* is a quote from Ryan Gosling, from the article, "Michelle Williams & Ryan Gosling: Heart to Heart," by Lynn Hirschberg, *W*, 30 September 2010.

Epigraphs
The first epigraph comes from the novel *Exodus*, by Lars Iyer (New York: Melville House, 2013).

The second epigraph is from the article, "The Mind-Bending Benedict Cumberbatch," by Michael Schulman, *Vanity Fair*, 4 October 2016.

The third epigraph is a quote from Gareth Wrighton, from the article, "Gareth Wrighton is Making Clothes for the Post-Truth Present," by Bryony Stone, *Dazed*, 9 July 2019.

Once You Push the Button

Epigraph
This quote from Ryan Gosling comes from the article, "Ryan Gosling is Hollywood's Handsomest, Wittiest, Leadingest Leading Man," by Chris Heath, *GQ*, 12 December 2016.

My little self repair

The second half of the second stanza quotes Ryan Gosling from the article, "Ryan Gosling is Hollywood's Handsomest, Wittiest, Leadingest Leading Man," by Chris Heath, *GQ*, 12 December 2016.

Where the f— are you?

The lines in opening stanza quote Warren Beatty, from the article "Six Decades In, Warren Beatty Is Still Seducing Hollywood," by Sam Kashner, *Vanity Fair*, 6 October 2016.

She reads Dan Brown

The fourth stanza quotes Rebecca Miller, from the article "Rebecca Miller Hates the Word "Brunch" but Loves *The Hills*," by David Kamp, *Vanity Fair*, 18 May 2016.

Let's Talk Sweatpants

For Neil Armstrong

The third stanza quotes Ryan Gosling, from the article, "Ryan Gosling is Hollywood's Handsomest, Wittiest, Leadingest Leading Man," by Chris Heath, *GQ*, 12 December 2016.

For Nicholas Cage

The last two lines from the second-last stanza are quoted from the article, "Sensible Mode," by Kevin Sintumuang, *Esquire*, 1 September 2018.

A clutter of memorabilia

The third stanza quotes Jim Jarmusch, from the article "Jim Jarmusch in Conversation with Adam Driver," by Christina Newland, *Dazed*, 12 July 2019.

A Thinking–woman's Fetish Object

Epigraph
This quote is from the novel *American Psycho*, by Bret Easton Ellis (New York: Random House, 1991).

Miserable while laughing

The first stanza quotes Ryan Gosling from the article, "Ryan Gosling," by Steve Carell, *Interview*, 7 October 2010.

The second last stanza quotes from the article, "The Most Stylish Sneakers to Wear With a Suit," by William Buckley, *Men's Journal*, Fall 2018.

A very un-moonlike rain

The final stanza quotes Scott Kelly's memoir, *Endurance*, as published in the article, "Space Odyssey," *National Geographic*, August 2017.

Acknowledgements

My thanks to Aritha van Herk, Brian Scrivener, Melina Cusano, Alison Cobra, and everyone at the University of Calgary Press for their work on this book. My thanks especially to Helen Hajnoczky for her poetic eye and editorial acumen. Thank you for the ongoing, unwavering support: Gillan Bohnet, Tasnuva Hayden, Tyler Hayden, and Natalie Simpson. And to all those whose presence in my life has given them a curious kind of presence in this book, I give my thanks.

Photo by Lily Wong

PAUL ZITS is a Calgary-based poet and teacher. He is the author of *Exhibit*, which won the Robert Kroetsch Award for Poetry, *Massacre Street*, winner of the Stephan G. Stephansson Award for Poetry, and *Leap-Seconds*, winner of the Robert Kroetsch Award for Innovative Poetry.

BRAVE & BRILLIANT SERIES

SERIES EDITOR:
Aritha van Herk, Professor, English, University of Calgary
ISSN 2371-7238 (PRINT) ISSN 2371-7246 (ONLINE)
Brave & Brilliant encompasses fiction, poetry, and everything in between and beyond. Bold and lively, each with its own strong and unique voice, Brave & Brilliant books entertain and engage readers with fresh and energetic approaches to storytelling and verse.

No. 1 · *The Book of Sensations* | Sheri-D Wilson

No. 2 · *Throwing the Diamond Hitch* | Emily Ursuliak

No. 3 · *Fail Safe* | Nikki Sheppy

No. 4 · *Quarry* | Tanis Franco

No. 5 · *Visible Cities* | Kathleen Wall and Veronica Geminder

No. 6 · *The Comedian* | Clem Martini

No. 7 · *The High Line Scavenger Hunt* | Lucas Crawford

No. 8 · *Exhibit* | Paul Zits

No. 9 · *Pugg's Portmanteau* | D. M. Bryan

No. 10 · *Dendrite Balconies* | Sean Braune

No. 11 · *The Red Chesterfield* | Wayne Arthurson

No. 12 · *Air Salt* | Ian Kinney

No. 13 · *Legislating Love* | Play by Natalie Meisner, with Director's Notes by Jason Mehmel, and Essays by Kevin Allen and Tereasa Maillie

No. 14 · *The Manhattan Project* | Ken Hunt

No. 15 · *Long Division* | Gil McElroy

No. 16 · *Disappearing in Reverse* | Allie McFarland

No. 17 · *Phillis* | Alison Clarke

No. 18 · *DR SAD* | David Bateman

No. 19 · *Unlocking* | Amy LeBlanc

No. 20 · *Spectral Living* | Andrea King

No. 21 · *Happy Sands* | Barb Howard

No. 22 · *In Singing, He Composed a Song* | Jeremy Stewart

No. 23 · *I Wish I Could be Peter Falk* | Paul Zits